Elena Tecchiati

Stereotyping leadership

An investigation about leaders' perception

Anchor Compact

Tecchiati, Elena: Stereotyping leadership: An investigation about leaders' perceptio, Hamburg, Anchor Academic Publishing 2015
Original title of the thesis: Gender and cultural differences in leader's perception

Buch-ISBN: 978-3-95489-360-7
PDF-eBook-ISBN: 978-3-95489-860-2
Druck/Herstellung: Anchor Academic Publishing, Hamburg, 2015

Bibliografische Information der Deutschen Nationalbibliothek:
Die Deutsche Nationalbibliothek verzeichnet diese Publikation in der Deutschen Nationalbibliografie; detaillierte bibliografische Daten sind im Internet über http://dnb.d-nb.de abrufbar

Bibliographical Information of the German National Library:
The German National Library lists this publication in the German National Bibliography. Detailed bibliographic data can be found at: http://dnb.d-nb.de

© Anchor Academic Publishing, ein Imprint der Diplomica® Verlag GmbH
http://www.diplom.de, Hamburg 2015
Printed in Germany

To my mother Elisabetta

and to my mentor Carlos María Moreno Pérez

Table of content

Summary

The objective of this study is to evaluate the gender and cultural differences in the perception of a male and a female leader in a feedback situation. The research will be based upon considerations of a literature review in the fields of gender bias and stereotype conducted previously. Subjects from Spain and Germany were asked to evaluate a director (male or female) of a fictive feedback situation that was described before a short questionnaire. The questions of the questionnaire were based on previous research and findings of the literature review. Results show no significance differences in the evaluation across genders and cultures. We tested if previous experience with a woman leader was related to a higher evaluation of the female leader finding no significant relationship. We tested if there was a relationship between the previous experience with a female leader and the preference to work for a certain leader's gender finding no significant relationship. Taking into consideration the subgroup "previous experience with a female leader", we analyzed if personnel responsibility was related to the preference to work for a certain leader's gender finding no relationship. Results from the study show that gender, culture and previous experience with a female leader had no influence on the leader's evaluation. A discussion with possible interpretations of the findings and implication for further research follows.

Introduction

The aim of this study is to give specific answers to questions in the field of differences in perception of a female leader in an intercultural setting. Gender bias defines the unequal treatment of women in employment opportunity and expectations due to their gender (Jamieson, 1996; Sandberg, 2013). In other words, people behave in a different way if they are dealing with a man or with a woman. When it comes to promotions and negotiations of salary, studies show that people prefer a man (Sandberg, 2013). Several studies underline this founding and give form to the phenomena called "glass ceiling" (Contreras Torres, Pedraza Ortiz, & Mejia Restrepo, 2012; Yukl, 2011, pp. 466-467). There is little or no research until now that this researcher has seen which has the gender bias as objective using a specific communication situation in an intercultural setting. This investigation will aim to capture intercultural differences in the perception of a feedback situation if held by a male or female leader. The questions that will be answered will cover: Do people from different nationalities perceive the same leader in the same situation in different ways? Do they perceive a leader differently if the leader is male or female? Is there a significant difference in like/dislike of one of the two genders in function of the gender and of the nationality of the test persons? Is there any difference in liking a leader depending on the gender or nationality of the people who give their evaluation?

The low number of women in charge of high-level leadership positions in different types of organizations suggests a widespread discrimination against women: 21.3% of the seats in parliaments globally are held by women (Inter-Parliamentary Union, 2013); in December 2012, 17 out of 195 independent countries in the world were led by women (CIA, 2012); 4.2 % of the Fortune 500 in 2012 were women (Sellers, 2012); leading women in scientific fields are outnumbered by men (Hill, Corbett, & Rose, 2010). Generally the numbers show a gradual increasing tendency in the last years, but still very few women hold high executive positions in large business organizations (Catalyst, 2003; Contreras Torres et al., 2012; Guzman & Rodriguez, 2008; Powell & Graves, 2003; Ragins, Townsend, & Mattis, 1998) and most of them who have reached the peak have reported that they have suffered from discrimination on their way up through the organization (Sandberg, 2013). This discrimination seems to be stronger in male-dominated industries (Gardiner & Tiggemann, 1999). The role and effects of "gender bias" is present in every workplace and organization (Jamieson, 1996; Sandberg, 2013). Women are, as a consequence, trapped in a "double bind", a psychological impasse and dilemma in communication that is created when an individual or a group receives two or more incongruent and conflictive messages, one of which negates the other (Bateson, Jackson, Haley, & Weakland, 1956). In this way a situation is created where the successful response to one message results in a failed response to the other (and vice versa). In this way the person will automatically be wrong regardless of response. The double bind occurs when the person cannot face and cope with the inherent dilemma, and therefore can neither resolve it nor back out of the dilemmatic situation (Bateson et al., 1956; Jamieson, 1995). As described by Bateson et al. (1956) the "double bind" refers to "a situation in which, no matter what a person does, he or she "can't win" (p. 251). Due to the stereotypical perception of women in an organization, this means that whatever women do, they can do no right, so that as a result, men are preferred for leadership positions and as a result it is very hard for a woman to climb up the ladder of success (Catalyst, 2007). The tendency to prefer men to women when it comes to fill top leadership positions is called "glass ceiling" (Segerman-Peck, 1991; Yukl, 2011, pp. 466-467). One explanation for the glass ceiling is the biased belief that women do not possess the skills necessary to lead effectively as these skills are viewed as typically masculine (Schein, 1975; Stogdill, 1974). "For a long time, women were assumed to be unable or unwilling to use the masculine behaviors considered essential for effective leadership" (Yukl, 2011, p.

467). In other words, the feminine stereotype shows a figure distant from the leader model mostly accepted by the many cultures and seems to be the principal cause for the glass ceiling effect (Contreras Torres et al., 2011). This is perceived by more than 85% of female leaders as the most important barrier on the way to higher positions in an organization (Catalyst, 2006). Several authors (Ragins et al., 1998; Schein, 2001; Tharenou, Latimer, & Conroy, 1994) suggested other reasons for the "glass ceiling" theory like: lack of visibility in the organization; lack of action by managers responsible for ensuring equal opportunity; bias to promote other managers similar to the managers taking the selection decision; higher standards of performance for women; lack of opportunity for effective mentoring programs; exclusion of women from informal communication programs that can offer promotion opportunities; lack of strong effort to be promoted or to obtain higher executive positions; demanding family situations; intentional efforts by some men to control and retain for themselves the best and more powerful leadership positions. Further studies show that women are less likely to ask for promotion and initiate a negotiation that can favor them (Babcock & Laschever, 2003) and that they have limited access to formal and informal networks in the organization (Bell & Nkomo, 2001). These explanations show a combination of factors that make the climate in an organization inhospitable and almost hostile for a woman. This situation is even worse if an organization has had previously a man in power so that a male-style interaction has been established as a norm (Tannen, 1996). Sandberg (2013) argues that these behaviors are the consequences of a stereotypical perception. In other words, women behave in a certain way because people do not let them behave in any another way. If they do, for example they behave more aggressively or more directive, they are said to be bad leaders. This is known as the Double-Bind-trap (Jamieson, 1995; Sandberg, 2013; Catalyst, 2007). Hollander and Yoder (1980) explained via a research review that the role expectations, style, and task demands of particular situations are responsible for the differences in the leadership behavior perception between men and women. In a survey

conducted in 1985, most managers (male and female) thought that women have to be

exceptional to have success in business and that women had a pessimistic view about their

chances in the workforce because they thought that they have to struggle more in order to

succeed and that their wage will be smaller than their male counterparts (Sutton & Moore,

1985). The last factor is called the "vertical division of labor", that refers to the inequality in

status and in pay between man and women and precisely it argues that women on average

earn less money than men even though they are exercising the same profession with the

same or better outcomes (Babcock et al., 2003; Blau & Kahn, 2007; Burr, 2003; Fernandez,

2006; Jamieson, 1995; Maruani, 1993; Moen, 1995). In the related "horizontal division of

labor" careers, jobs and professions are gendered so that some jobs are seen more female-

relevant and others more male-relevant and in many companies the sexes are segregated

according to their positions. For example, women's jobs are seen as supportive and caring

(such as secretary, nursery school teachers and nurses) and men's jobs are seen more

directive (such as electronic engineers, managers and programmers) (Bass, 2008, p. 903;

Burr, 2003; Maruani, 1993). An interaction of the horizontal and vertical divisions interact

such that men, entering a job career that is associated with women, are likely to ascend

higher and more quickly to a leading position (Burr, 2003). According to Kling (1975) there

is a positive correlation between testosterone levels and aggression. Persky, Smith, and Basu

(1971) found a positive correlation between aggressive and hostile behavior testing a sample

of men. According to these studies women's lack of assertiveness and aggression is the

reason why they do not ascend and may avoid the senior well-paid jobs (Burr, 2003).

Aggressiveness is the clearest difference identified by Maccoby and Jacklin (1974). In this

study the researchers reviewed the results of several studies in the field of gender

differences. They concluded that women and men differ in other 3 areas: mathematical abilities (boys overtake girls more or less at the age of 12) visual-spatial abilities (boys are better than girls in embedded figure tests, frame tests and identifying rotated figures); verbal abilities (girls show more competence in fluency, creative writing and comprehension). Other differences are due to the environmental influences of parents and other interacting persons that according to their stereotypical perception treat boys and girls in a different way (Codry & Codry, 1976).

In this context Eagly (1987) suggests the "social role theory". This theory recognizes the historical division in labor between women (often assuming responsibilities at home) and men (assuming responsibilities outside of the home). According to this hypothesis the expectations of women and men are dependent and related to the sex differences in social behavior and such expectations are transmitted to future generations influencing the behavior and expectancies of each gender (Eagly, 1987, 1997; Eagly, Wood, & Diekman, 2000). As consequence the behavior of women and men is strongly influenced by the stereotypes of their social roles. The theory can explain the difference in perception of a male or a female leader and the reasons why it is difficult for a woman to ascend in male dominated labor worlds (Godoy & Mladinic, 2009). Other consequences of the differences just mentioned above reveal differences in communication and leadership styles (Contreras Torres et al., 2011; Tannen, 1994, 1996). This does not mean that women are worse leaders than the male counterparts (Sandberg, 2013).

Women and transformational leadership

Some studies reported that the outcome of the female and male leadership styles had no significant difference (Judeh, 2010; Manning, 2002). A study by Eagly, Johannesen-Schmidt, and Van Engen, (2002) showed instead that female leaders were rated by their subordinates as being more transformational leaders than male leaders. The study consisted of a meta-analysis of 45 studies of transformational, transactional, and laissez-faire leadership styles.

The transformational leadership theory was described by Bass & Avolio (1994) and consists in a concept of leadership as "exceptional leadership performance that exist when leaders broaden and elevate the interests of their followers, when they generate awareness and acceptance of the purposes and mission of the group, and when those leaders stir their followers to look beyond their self-interest for the group benefit" (Judeh, 2010, p. 1-2).

Bass & Avolio (1994) explain in the Full Range Leadership Theory (FRLT) that every leader should use different styles of leadership in order to be effective. The different styles can be summarized as following: Laissez-faire leadership style: the leader is absent and let the subordinates decide; Management by exception: the leader intervene shortly before or after a mistake has made by subordinates; Transactional leadership: leader and subordinates exchange e.g. services, work, development program with wage, free time or praise; Transformational leadership: inspires and motivates through effective communication, through her charismatic power, through positive interactions and positive influence.

In order to measure the perception of a leader by his followers according to the Full Range Leadership Theory (Avolio, 2011), the researchers mentioned above (Judeh, 2010; Manning, 2002; Eagly et al., 2010), used the MLQ (multifactor leadership questionnaire), a tool developed by Bass and Avolio (2000) selves. The MLQ is a questionnaire similar to a 360° questionnaire, which is sent, usually electronically, to various employees and supervisors of the executive who is being assessed, and completed by those persons. The completed questionnaires are returned electronically to the institution that is doing the evaluation. A copy is filled out by the executive himself or herself, the so-called Self-Score Version. The evaluation is also sent electronically, and a profile of the executive is created.

The concept of transformational leadership shows a type of leader that is valued as effective, well accepted and admired, and that it represents a role model because of their inspirational and charismatic characteristics (Bass & Avolio, 1994; Bass & Riggio, 2006; Yukl, 2011). Results of the research program GLOBE confirm that the transformational leadership style is valued positively and effectively by every country and culture (Dorfman, Hanges, & Brodbeck, 2004). The study by Eagly et al. (2003), mentioned above, shows contradictory results with other studies that suggest clearly that female leaders in the workplace are less liked than their male colleagues even though they are perceived as competent (Catalyst, 2007). The transformational leader in fact is liked and respected, is seen as social and empathetic and has high interpersonal competences such as social skills. Social skills include, for example, empathy and communication abilities and leaders help their subordinates satisfy their personal needs (Hall & Donnell, 1979; Hogan & Hogan, 2002). That is why a female leader can fast relate to others and as a consequence could advance faster in her career (Hall & Donnell, 1979). Nevertheless recent studies that analyze the different types of leadership shown by women and men, report that women leaders tend to show a more transformational leadership style, the most effective style in an organization (Eagly & Carli, 2004, 2007; García-Retamero & López-Zafra, 2006).

Conflicting stereotypes

The tendency of the interpretation of sex-related stereotypes in management and leadership is showing a slow positive change in favor of the perception for women leaders. A comparison of surveys about the perception of women in business showed that managers' perception has changed enormously in favor of women (Sutton & Moore, 1985). A recent poll conducted in August 2013 by Gallup - Gallup's annual Work and Education survey (Newport, & Wilke, 2013) showed that 35% of the interviewed Americans (independently of their working status and of the gender) prefer to have a man as boss, and 23% prefer to have a woman as a boss and 41% declared that it makes no difference if they have a woman or a man as a boss. A comparison made also by Gullop (Newport & Wilke, 2013) using the same survey that has been repeated almost every year since 1953 showed an increased tendency in preferring a woman as a boss, and a decrease tendency in preferring a man. In 1953 only 5% preferred a female boss, 66% a male boss and 25% said that it did not make a difference. One reason for this trend is suggested by the fact that in the survey of 2013 the preference for a female boss was higher among those people that at the time of the survey were working for a woman. This result suggests that the contact with female leaders could distort the stereotypical perception that a woman cannot be a good leader. Another reason could be that as more women are working in higher directive roles, people who were working for them at the time of the survey were experiencing them as better leaders than the men they had as a boss before the survey. The stereotypical image people have of a woman does not fit the directive role of a leader and as a consequence they do not think women are suitable in performing higher positions in a company (Bass, 2008, p.906; Bem, 1970; Bowman, Worthy, & Greyser, 1965; Burr, 2003). Further, women are generally considered to be too emotional and submissive to be effective leaders, aggressive "workaholic" and manipulative (Heller, 1982). Hence, the stereotypical concepts of "woman" and "leader" may be incompatible (Schein, 1973, 1975). Kruse and Wintermantel (1986) found in a study with male students that the concept of "man" has a correlation of .9 with the concept of "manager" and .8 with the concept of "leadership". On the contrary the concept of "woman" showed a correlation of -.4 with the concept of "manager" and .5 with the concept of "leadership". The beliefs that a female leader makes a "worse" leader are also common among women (O'Leary, 1974; McLelland, 1965). In a study of women in leadership positions in the fields of science and technology the difficulties arising in a man dominated world were evaluated. The study reported that, in order to be recognized as a "leader", they had to assume some specific types of characteristics, such as aggression, authority, harder and strong character, characteristics normally associated with men (Yañez & Godoy, 2008).

In a dissertation study Seifert (1984) showed the power of stereotypical beliefs. Seifert let male and female participants think that they were working with female and male leaders and that the leaders were selected randomly. In the truth they were receiving the same standardized communication messages from the experimenter. The participants who thought they were receiving directions from a male leader evaluated the communication clearer and the female leaders were rated less fairly selected than were male leaders (Seifert, 1984). In the study it is not mentioned if the boss is seen as more competent or more empathetic. It would be also interesting to test differences among cultures as the study reflects the thoughts of Americans (like the most studies mentioned above).

Another must recent study conducted by Godoy & Mladinic (2009) investigates the perception of leaders offering a description of an efficient, competent and successful leader. The description was offered in two dimensions, giving a male and a female leader. The testing individuals had the task to evaluate the person through questions using a Likert scale from 1 to 7. The dependent variables were divided into labor (leadership effectiveness; task orientation; interpersonal orientation; cognitive skills; recommendations about organizational recompense; salary and promotion) and personal issues (general evaluation as person; pleasant and sympathy level; if they would ask the person for support of advice in case of personal problems; if they would establish a friendship with this person). The results showed no significant difference in the evaluation, in other words "neither the participant's nor the target's sex influenced evaluations" (Godoy & Mladinic, 2009, p. 51). The male leader did not receive better evaluation than the female leader. In the study Godoy & Mladinic (2009) do not report if the testing persons have already had experiences working with a female leader, as reported by the Gullop survey (Newport & Wilke, 2013) explained above.

After a review of the literature and of the studies in the field of stereotypical perceptions the question about how people feel about a male or female leader in a specific situation was not conclusive. The study by Seifert (1984) offers a way of answering, in a vague manner, the above question but as the study is almost 30 years old. Additionally, as reflected in the Gullop poll (Newport & Wilke, 2013) already mentioned, the tendency of how people see a woman as a leader is changing so that, from the point of view of this study, a new research in the area is required. The study by Godoy & Mladinic (2009) offers a more positive view about how people perceive a male and a female leader, but the study shows only a description, not a communication interaction between the leader and other actors (for example other employees). Most difficulties that women have in ascending a male dominated world happen during interactions with other people who can be responsible for a higher position. As described by several communication experts (Lay, 1978; Pearce & Cronen, 2006; Schulz von Thun, 2010; Schulz von Thun, Ruppel, & Stratmann, 2000; Watzlawick, 2005) social reality is created through the way we see our interactions with others and through the words and sentences we use to communicate with each other. The description offered by Godoy & Mladinic (2009) is a static one without offering any interaction. Communication skills and competences are basic to leadership (Barge & Hirokawa, 1989) and they are the most important parameters in order to assess the perception of a leader. Moreover "quality and style of a leader's communication to followers makes a difference in the success and effectiveness of the leadership" (Bass, 2008, p. 125).

In conclusion, the questions of differences in perception about communication competences, effectiveness and respect have not been answered concretely in the past. However, they should, as they form part of the effective leadership model according to the theory of the transformational leadership mentioned above (Avolio, 2011; Bass, 2008). A specific communication situation offers a concrete basis to determine the differences in perceptions. It would be useful to see if the perception shows any difference among different nationalities and cultures. After a profound review of the literature there it is surmised that no study has been conducted concerning the differences in perception of female leaders between different or some European countries using a specific communication situation.

Several studies show that women of different cultures have reported similar experiences of barriers to their ascent in a company and reveal that among different cultures there are similarities in the way women are seen (Catalyst, 2006). A more thorough review of the literature suggests though that in some cultures gender stereotyping is stronger than in others (Catalyst, 2006). Specifically, it depends on the egalitarian values lived in a Country: Where gender equality is an ideal and is lived as a value, feminine stereotypic traits are more highly regarded in societies with less egalitarian values and norms (Emrich, Denmark, & Den Hartog, 2004). On the other side of the spectrum, where gender equality is not valued, gender stereotyping is less strong (Emrich et al., 2004). The Cultural Perspectives Questionnaire (CPQ) is a validated tool that assesses individuals' preferences, attitudes and beliefs about how people should relate to each other and to the environment where they live and perform (Catalyst, 2006). In a study that measured culture using the tool CPQ, investigators statistically analyzed similarities and differences in the cultural preferences of different European countries. Figure 1 shows the results of the cultural similarities in clusters. Another study in the past has shown similar results (Gupta, Hanges, & Dorfman, 2002).

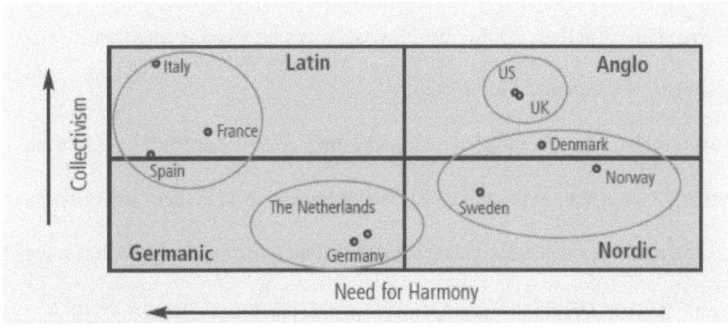

Figure 1. Clusters of culturally similar countries (Catalyst, 2007).

As shown in Figure 1 the authors defined collectivism (underlying the group belonging rather than individuality) and harmony (preference for living in balance with the environment) as the dimensions that best describe the differences among cultures and that in this way European countries can be divided into clusters (see Figure 1). The position of Germany shows a less collectivist culture where harmony plays a less important role than in Spain. This comparison could suggest that in a Germanic culture (less collectivist and less need for harmony) the female stereotype (in need for harmony and more collectivist than men, according to gender stereotype studies) is not as strong as in Spain. In this context it is worth noting that the German Chancellor Angela Merkel has been in power since 2005, and is presently the only woman in power for so long worldwide (Connolly & Oltermann, 2013), and this may have an impact on German culture. In this context it is also important to mention that after the Second World War German women rebuilt German towns and cities (the so called "Trummerfrauen"). Many men during this period were kept as prisoners of war or had died. Women, therefore, had significant responsibility for the rebuilding of the German economy (Arnold, 1999). This also might have affected German culture and the way women are perceived in the workplace. Taking into consideration the difference/similarity shown in the above study (Catalyst, 2006), the question arises on whether there is a difference between a Germanic and a Latin culture.

Other questions that arise after the literature and study review are: "Is a woman seen less transformational than a man in the same effective situation? And is there any difference of perceiving an executive woman among the cultures? Is she more or less liked than a man? If a person has already worked with a female leader, would this person again work for a female leader? In other words: can a strong and common stereotype be erased through experience?"

Hypothesis

The review of the literature about stereotypes and female leaders as reported above was the base of different thoughts and reflections that resulted in three different hypotheses for the present investigation:

1. The male leader receives a more positive evaluation than the female leader across cultures and gender;

2. In the case of previous experience with a female leader and at the same time evaluating the feedback situation where a woman is acting as a director, individuals tend to evaluate the female leader higher than the male counterpart when individuals have no previous experience with a female leader;

3. There is a relationship between previous experience and the preference for a leader of a certain gender: previous experience with a woman leader means higher preference to work with a female leader.

Method

Overview

In order to test the hypotheses listed above a method was developed that gave the researchers the possibility to gather a relatively large amount of data in a short time (we had about 35 days at our disposal). This meant taking into consideration the economic factor of the study offering a method that was less time intensive for the respondents. Considering the fact that we wanted individuals to evaluate a leader in a communication situation as already discussed we developed a written fictive situation of a feedback situation between a director and an employee. A small questionnaire with six items and some demographic questions followed. Because of the researchers personal and professional relationships with Germany and residence in Barcelona (Spain) an evaluation tool was developed for both countries - Germany and Spain. The original instrument was first developed in English, validated by three leadership experts, by two communication experts and by two statistic professors. After the validation process it was translated into German and Spanish.

In the following sections the two parts of the tool (the feedback situation and the questionnaire) are described.

The feedback situation

We chose to let evaluate a feedback situation because after Bass (2008) "feedback about subordinate's performance is the most common contingent reinforcement provided by a leader" (p. 402) and it belongs to the most important and basic tasks of a leader (Felfe, 2009; Niermeyer & Postall, 2008) and it offers the chance to improve the quality of human relationships (Folkman, 2006). The feedback was described after the communication tools of Marshall Rosenberg, (2010; 2011):

- Observing without judging;

- Expressing feelings, not thought;

- Expressing needs, not strategies;

- Making concrete and clear requests.

The "nonviolent communication", after Rosenberg, offers a precise and assertive way to communicate, respecting needs and the needs of the communication partner. This is strongly human oriented and enhances relationships through empathy, mutual understanding, trust and cooperation (Rosenberg, 2010, 2011). According to a study by Vries, Bakker-Pieper, and Oostenveld (2009) human oriented communication is seen as one of the communication styles of effective leadership. Using the nonviolent communication steps in the communication routine helps to improve performance, reduce conflicts and enhance relationships (Rosenberg, 2003). Furthermore, other characteristics were added to the feedback situation described according to Niermeyer and Postall (2008, pp. 50-51):

- Do not judge the person but the behavior/situation;

- Describe without interpreting;

- Give examples and be concrete;

- Praise positive aspects of the situation/behavior;

- Thank the subordinate for the feedback, for the time and for the acceptance;

- Help to find solutions;

- Use a "partner" language (use "we" instead of "you");

- Ask for self-evaluation and evaluation of the situation.

The feedback was written first in English by the investigator and afterwards validated by three experienced executives with international background and two communication experts. In this way the feedback was assured to mirror a communication situation of a high transformational leader with long experience. The fictive leader of the situation is a director of sales of a fictive company that gives feedback to a subordinate who has not reached the yearly goals though the offers of support by the director in the past months.

After the validation 4 dimensions were developed for the feedback. Crossing the gender of the leader and of the subordinate in order to check the possible difference of perception due to differences in gender of the subordinate and leader:

1. Male leader X male subordinate (MM)

2. Male leader X female subordinate (MF)

3. Female leader X male subordinate (FM)

4. Female leader X female subordinate (FF)

The questionnaire

After the feedback situation six specific evaluation questions followed: The first four questions come from the Multifactor Leadership Questionnaire (MLQ, 2000). These are the questions 21 ("The person I am evaluating acts in ways that builds my respect"), 23 ("The person I am evaluating acts in ways that builds my respect") and 25 ("The person I am evaluating displays a sense of power and confidence") that belong to the dimension "Idealized influence" and the question 38 ("The person I am evaluating uses methods of leadership that are satisfying") that belongs to the dimension "Inspirational Motivation – Satisfaction" in the MLQ. These specific questions were chosen because they apply to the situation and in order to give a qualitative evaluation of the leader. The original MLQ's likert scale was changed because originally it considered how often the leader behaves in a certain way (Not at all / Once in a while / sometimes / fairly often / frequently, if not always). This was changed to "I strongly disagree / I do not agree / Neither agree nor disagree / I agree / I strongly agree" because a specific situation was being considered.

Two other questions followed in order to measure if the test sample liked the leader in the feedback situation ("I like the boss and the way the boss acts and communicates" and "I would like to work with this boss"). A question was added that takes a lead from the Gullop research from 1953 to 2013 (Newport & Wilke, 2013). This centered on obtaining information about the preference of a female or male leader in their future: "If you were taking a new job and had your choice of a boss would you prefer to work for a woman or for a man?" Three different answers were possible: For a man/For a Woman/Indifferent.

Among the demographic questions (age/gender/nationality/formation) another question was asked: had the testing person ever had personnel responsibility and following the research of the Gullop study mentioned above (Newport & Wilke, 2013) we asked if the evaluator has had previous experience with a female leader. Taking the last question into consideration eight dimensions were obtained for the questionnaire and 16 if the nationality or the cultural feedback is included (German/Spanish) (see Table 1).

Table 1

The questionnaire's dimensions for the study evaluation.

Dimension	Leader	Subordinate	Previous experience with a female leader	Cultural background
1	Male	Male	Yes	German
2	Male	Male	No	German
3	Male	Male	Yes	Spanish
4	Male	Male	No	Spanish
5	Male	Female	Yes	German
6	Male	Female	No	German
7	Male	Female	Yes	Spanish
8	Male	Female	No	Spanish
9	Female	Male	Yes	German
10	Female	Male	No	German
11	Female	Male	Yes	Spanish
12	Female	Male	No	Spanish
13	Female	Female	Yes	German
14	Female	Female	No	German
15	Female	Female	Yes	Spanish
16	Female	Female	No	Spanish

Procedures

After the validation of the feedback situation through different experts and the validation of the questions of the questionnaire and hypothesis by two statistic professors (Dr. Cifre, Faculty of Psychology University Blanquerna, Barcelona, Spain and Mr. Reyes, graduated in economics at the Universidad de Barcelona, Spain) the feedback and the questions were translated into German and Spanish. The German translation of the feedback situation was made by the initiator of the study between the 12th and 15th March and was validated by Matthias Moritz on the 18th March as German is his mother language and he already validated the original feedback in English. The translation into Spanish was made by an official translator from Madrid who has been living in Germany for more than 25 years. She received on the 4th March the English and the German version of the feedback situation in order to fit the two forms as perfect as possible. She sent the translation per Email on the 13th of March.

The questions by the MLQ were taken by the original validated questionnaires of the two languages (Spanish version of 2000 and German version of 2002).

After this step the four forms of the instrument (male leader / male employee; male leader / female employee; and so forth) adapting the feminine and masculine words depending on the gender of the leader were written out. The instrument (feedback and questionnaire) in two versions for every language were developed:

- a "paper-pencil" version using 3 pages (two for the feedback situation and one for the questionnaire);

- an online version using the tool "Google Drive" in exchange with the Blanquerna account of the study initiator. The online tool offered by Google in order to create an easy tool to read and to evaluate was utilized. No question could be left out. Google offers an excel table with the answers and date of filling.

Between 19th and 27th March 150 questionnaires were sent to Germany by ordinary mail to 11 contact persons in Germany. Every contact received between 10 and 20 questionnaires and had the task to distribute the questionnaires to Germans (or to people that have been living in Germany for many years) and who have had work experience. On the 18th March an online version of the German questionnaire was made and sent to 12 email addresses of colleagues of the study initiator.

Between the 25th March and 5th April 100 Spanish questionnaire were distributed per hand by the investigator. On the 20th of March the online form was written and sent per email to 10 different professionals known by the investigator.269 filled questionnaires were collected, including the online versions:

157 Questionnaires from Germany: 32 online and 125 paper-pencil versions.

112 Questionnaire from Spain: 21 online and 91 paper-pencil versions.

A questionnaire from Germany was received where six answers (three of the items and two of the demographic questions) were left out. This questionnaire could not be used. This questionnaire was not included in the investigation and we will analyze a total of 268 questionnaires.

In table 2 the numbers of questionnaires are summarized and divided into Country of origin, gender and dimensions.

Table 2:

Visualization of the questionnaires' structure received by country and dimension.

		MM		MF		FF		FM		Total
		1	*2*	*3*	*4*	*5*	*6*	*7*	*8*	
	Gender									
Spain	M	8	4	8	4	9	2	7	3	M 45
	F	9	2	11	3	11	4	20	7	F 67
Total		17	6	19	7	20	6	27	10	
			23		26		26		37	112
Germany	M	13	6	17	13	5	6	2	9	M 71
	F	13	5	13	8	14	3	14	15	F 85
Total		26	11	30	21	19	9	16	24	
			37		51		28		40	156
Total		43	17	49	28	39	15	43	34	
			60		77		54		77	**268**

Participants

The subjects that evaluated the feedback situation came from different working fields and were living in Germany and in Spain. The questionnaires were delivered to professionals living in Germany (German questionnaire) and in Spain (Spanish version) and who were able to distribute them to people living and working in their environment. In this way a significant number of students and scholars were excluded and people with no experience dealing with managers and executives. The questionnaire was distributed in different working fields such as:

- Consulting sector

- Marketing and advertising

- Consumer industry

- Construction industry

- Public sector

- Health management

- Health industry
- Education.

Different working levels from internship to director and executive levels were covered in the research. Due to the amount of questionnaires and to the irregular answers received it is not possible to declare exactly how many questionnaires come from which economic sectors.

The age of the evaluators ranged between 18 and 80. The average was 41.96 years and the median was 42.5 years.

Not all the subjects were Germans and Spanish. Among the questionnaires coming from Germany we found a subject coming from Austria and one coming from Hungary. The last one reported that his mother language was Hungarian and not German. The other subjects reported to be German and German as their mother language.

Among the questionnaires coming from Spain we found one subject coming from Portugal, two from France, one from Poland, one from Morocco, one from the United States of America and one person was Italian/Venezuelan. Only the last one reported Spanish as their mother language.

Among the questionnaires coming from Spain 33 persons reported Catalan as their mother language. As in Barcelona, Catalonia, Spain, both languages Catalan and Spanish are official and people born in Barcelona tend to be raised with the two languages, we did not considerate this as a sign for a different culture.

Results

The evaluation of the questionnaires was made through the computer program for statistics SPSS. A pre-analysis of the dependent variable and then stratified per gender's subjects gave abnormal distribution so that a non-parametric method: U-Mann-Whitney was applied.

In the hypothesis 1 the male leader was assumed to receive a more positive evaluation that the female leader across cultures and gender. The maximum points that could be given to a leader was 30 (5 points of the Likert scale for each of the 6 items) was considered. As p .974 (> .05) it can be assumed that the gender of the leader had no influence on the evaluation and so the evaluations show no significance difference if the director was female or male.

Taking into consideration only the cultures, i.e. the origin of the questionnaires, it was found that there was no significance difference: p .483 (> .05) considering only the questionnaires coming from Spain and p .947 (> .05) if considering the questionnaires coming from Germany. It can be assumed that culture had no influence on the evaluation because both cultures tended to evaluate the two genders of the feedback in the same manner.

Taking into consideration the genders of the subjects, as to say of the evaluators, it was found there was no significant difference. Female subjects tended to evaluate male and female directors with no difference (p .460 > .05) as well as the male subjects (p .832 > .05).

In the second hypothesis previous experience with a female leader was considered, assuming that the subjects reporting a previous experience with a female leader, tended to evaluate the feedback situation, where the director was female, better than individuals who were evaluating the male director reporting no previous experience with a female leader. The results reported no significant difference: subjects with previous experience with a female leader did not tend to evaluate the female director better than subjects that evaluated a male director having no previous experience with a female leader (p .111 > .05). We analyzed as well the difference between the evaluations of the female subjects with previous experience with a female leader who evaluated the female director, with the group of the female subjects with previous experience with a female leader who evaluated the male director. Still in this case we found no significant difference (p .827 > .05) so that we can assume generally that previous experience with a female leader had no influence on the evaluations.

Preference to work for a specific gender

In the third hypothesis a relationship between previous experience and the preference for a leader of a certain gender was assumed, so that previous experience with a female boss signifies higher preference to work with a female leader. Taking into consideration all questionnaires: 19,78% of the subjects (53 out of 268) reported they would prefer to work for a man, 8,95% (24 out of 268) prefer to work for a woman, and 71.27% (191 out of 268) reported no preference. Regarding the questionnaires coming from Germany: 21.80% of the subjects (34) prefer to work for a male leader (21 women and 13 men), 8.89% (14) prefer to work for a female leader (8 women and 6 men), and 69.23% (108) reported no difference of preference. Regarding the questionnaires coming from Spain: 16.96% (19) prefer to work for a male leader (7 women and 11 men), 16.07% (18) of the subjects reported a preference for a female leader (11 woman and 8 men), and 66.97% (75) expressed no preference.

Analyzing the data for the third hypothesis the method of the Chi-Squared-Test was used and it was found that there was no significant relationship between the preference of a specific leader's gender and the previous experience with a female leader (p .799 > .05). These data suggest that the previous experience had no influence on the evaluations and in this precise case on the preference to work for a man or for a woman. The group of the subjects with previous experience with a female leader was analyzed in more depth. It was assumed that a further relationship could be elucidated so the demographic data was analyzed. Considering only the group of subjects reporting previous experience with a female leader (180 subjects), and dividing this group into three subgroups (preference to work for a man, preference to work for a woman, indifferent) and taking into consideration the two subgroups "Preference for a man" and "Preference for a woman" it was not found, at first glance, any significant difference in the age groups (average of 41.96 and 41.87 years respectively) and in the educational level average (2.79 and 2.78 respectively offering a Likert scale 1-4 in the questionnaire). Analysis of the relationship between the personnel responsibility and the preference for a certain gender was performed. It was assumed in this case that the experience with the two genders as an executive should not influence the preference to work for a certain gender. The data suggest that there is no significant difference (p .801 > .05). That is to say there is no relationship between personnel responsibility and the preference for a certain gender's leader. As well it was found no relationship between personnel responsibility and the preference for a certain gender's leader when taking into consideration the subgroup "No preference" as well (p .813 > .05).

Discussion

The results suggested that all three hypotheses were not confirmed. The results in this study demonstrate that the cultural background was not the reason for differences in perception although a review of the literature showed other conclusions as already described. Barcelona is the capital of Catalonia and shows in general a less conservative point of view than the rest of Spain. The Catalan economy is the first in the ranking in the autonomous communities of Spain (INE, 2011) and could be an indicator for a different type of mentality maybe nearer to the one present in the northern European area. Further studies in perception of leaders and leadership could clarify if there is a significant difference between different parts of Spain. A deeper analysis of the cultural differences could be interesting also in order to determinate if the differences can be only at a superficial level, as to say that the open behavior of one culture does not respect what is actually thought.

The fact that there is no significant difference between the evaluations of a male and of a female director could have an impact on the decision of future trainings and developmental programs in leadership. The results suggest that a woman could have difficulties on her way "up" to higher hierarchical levels as already described in the introduction, but that her credibility and competence is taken for granted once she gets to the higher position. This point of view, could suggest two different views of seeing the glass ceiling effect: women that reach the higher level have specific competencies that according to the researches in the field of stereotype are similar to the male's competencies or (as a different option) only the women that are willing to go through a harder developmental program and are willing to "fight" more for their positions and sacrifice more time are getting there because they show to be better than their male counterpart (Sandberg, 2013; Sherwin, 2014). To confirm this theory though would require a long-term study to be tested. On the other hand, studies show that females lead in a more effective manner (Eagly & Carli, 2004, 2007; Sandberg, 2013;

Sherwin, 2014) not excluding the fact that women have to "fight" more to get there. It is worth noting that many women stop their career because of lack of support when they have children and experience more challenges climbing up their career ladders once they go back to work (Eagly & Carli, 2007; Sandberg, 2013). All these explanations do not exclude each other and are interrelated to each other hand research does not show a clear and unique view to the interpretation of the difficulties arising for a woman fighting against the gender bias effect. A proposal for a future study based on this investigation could be to create much more dimensions based on masculine and feminine type of leadership and investigating if the perception and likability of a leader changes according to these factors. In the future there should be more consideration concerning a feminine and a masculine way of leading instead of talking about men and women leaders.

The results of the analysis of the answers to the question "If you were taking a new job and had your choice of a boss would you prefer to work for a woman or for a man?" show a similar pattern to the results of the Gullop study (Newport & Wilke, 2013): A higher number of answers were in favor of a male leader. A larger intercultural sample could give more significance to the answer concerning this tendency. At the same time surveys on this theme should be repeated at regular basis in Europe in order to capture tendencies like the American study. It was found that the previous experience with a female leader had no impact on the results of the leader's evaluations showing opposite results of the Gullop study (Newport & Wilke, 2013). Further, it was found that no relationship between the previous experience with a female leader and the personnel responsibility reported by the subjects in the questionnaires. This finding could be explained If one assumed that executives (people in charge of personnel) are accustomed to managing two genders and their experience, in this sense, have no gender bias. Further studies, are therefore suggested. Though a more profound analysis of variables such as: level of hierarchy, the number of persons as subordinates and the years of experience of the leader.

It was also assumed though that some results left some questions open that could be answered analyzing the demographical data, but still they did not help to clarify some results. The fact that previous experience with a female leader did not influence the evaluation of the leader could suggest that the discussion about introducing the rule of hiring a certain amount of female in every company should be banned definitely. Offering more specific communication and inclusion developmental programs in and outside the organizations (not only for women but also for men) treating openly the gender bias and how to avoid it could give results more sustainable than hiring a woman just because "we have to". It can be argued that hiring a woman just because we need more women in organizations (and not because of a good CV, for example) can be demotivating because the female candidate who will get the job will not feel estimate as a working force. Further research should analyze the impact of such trainings and developmental programs as well as supportive programs for women who have to face the family and the working responsibility. As well informative programs for male leaders, for husband and for fathers who could take a more supportive role for their wives on their way up could be interesting developmental programs that need to be evaluated systematically.

Further questions about the best and most suitable way of giving feedback arise. Even though the feedback evaluation was not the direct object of this study further research should take also this aspect into consideration as well considering the feedback situation in a diversity organizational environment. The written situation showed its limits as it could not imply body posture and voice pitch, the most important part of our communication setting. Nonverbal communication tells, such as the way someone is sitting or looking at the speech partner, can give implicit messages that can change the meaning of a sentence. So for example a positive written sentence can become ironic or sarcastic just speaking it in a certain tone of voice (Collett, 2009; Ekman, 2005, 2009; Mehrabian 1981).

Conclusion

Even though the results did not confirm our previous analysis and hypothesis we opened ways to consider new research. Even though the glass ceiling may never be broken, it is expected that research and studies that can support and deliver new perspectives for trainings, developmental and support programs for women in order to clarify and explain the consequences of stereotyping enhancing inclusion. In this study it is confirmed how complex the field of gender bias is and that the questions about the reasons for the glass ceiling cannot be explained in any unique way.

Cultural differences should be analyzed in more depth as this could be helpful to understand the impact and development of the gender bias effect in other country.

The fact that a women stops working for a while in order to have children should not stay in opposition to the fact that breaking the glass ceiling is a matter that meets everybody's needs, as diversity in a company can bring creativity and different point of view which could enhance productivity (Sandberg, 2013).

New questions about the "perfect" feedback in a diverse organization arise and open new doors for new more complex investigations where the combination of different variables could give new insights in the educational and organizational settings.

References

Arnold, A.M. (1999). *Trümmerbahn und Trümmerfrauen*. Berlin: Omnis Verlag.

Avolio, B.J. (2011). *The full range leadership development*. Los Angeles: Sage.

Babcock, L., & Laschever, S. (2003). *Women don't ask: Negotiation and the gender divide*. Princeton, NJ: Princeton University Press.

Barge, J.K., & Hirokawa, R.Y. (1989). Towards a communication competency model of leadership. *Small Group Behavior, 20,* 167-189.

Bass B.M. (2008). *The Bass handbook of leadership*. New York: Free Press.

Bass, B.M., & Avolio, B.J. (1994). *Improving organizational effectiveness through transformational leadership*. Thousand Oaks: Sage.

Bass, B.M., & Avolio, B.J. (2000). *MLQ: Multifactor leadership questionnaire*. Redwood City, CA: Mind Garden.

Bass, B.M., & Riggio, R.E. (2006). *Transformational leadership*. New York: Psychology Press.

Bateson, G., Jackson, D. D., Haley, J., & Weakland, J. (1956). Towards a theory of schizophrenia. *Behavioral Science, 1,* 251–264

Bell, E.L., & Nkomo, S.M. (2001). *Our separate ways: Black and white women and the struggle for professional identity*. Boston: Harvard Business School Press.

Bem, D.J. (1979). *Beliefs, attitudes and human affairs*. Belmont, CA: Brooks/Cole.

Blau, F.D., & Kahn, L.M. (2007). The gender pay gap? Have women gone as far as they can? *Academy of Management Perspectives*, *21*, 7-23. Retrieved from https://www.stanford.edu/group/scspi/_media/pdf/key_issues/gender_research.pdf

Bowman, G.W., Worthy, N.B. & Greysers, S.A. (1965). Are women executive people? *Harvard Business Review*, 43(4).

Burr, V. (2003). *Gender and social psychology*. New York: Routledge.

Catalyst (2003). *Women in U.S. corporate leadership*. New York: Author published.
Retrieved from http://www.catalyst.org/system/files/Women_in_US_Corporate
_Leadership.pdf

Catalyst (2006). Different cultures, similar perceptions: stereotyping of western European
Business Leaders. New York: Catalyst Publication. Retrieved from
http://www.catalyst.org/system/files/Different_Cultures%2C_Similar_Perceptions_Stere
otyping_of_Western_European_Business_Leaders.pdf

Catalyst (2007). *The double-bind dilemma for women in leadership: damned if you do,
doomed if you don't*. New York: Author published. Retrieved from
http://www.catalyst.org/system/files/The_Double_Bind_Dilemma_for_Women_in_Lead
ership_Damned_if_You_Do_Doomed_if_You_Dont.pdf

CIA (2012). *Chief of State and Cabinet Members of Foreign Governments Directory*.
Retrieved from https://www.cia.gov/library/publications/world-leaders-
1/pdfs/2012/December2012ChiefsDirectory.pdf.

Codry J., & Codry S. (1976). Sex differences: a study of the eye of the beholder.
Childdevelopment, 47, 812-819.

Collett, P. (2007). *Ich sehe was, was du nicht sagst*. Bergisch Gladbach: Lübbe.

Connolly, K., & Oltermann, P. (2013). German election: Angela Merkel secures historic
third win. *The Guardian*. Retrieved from
http://www.theguardian.com/world/2013/sep/22/angela-merkel-wins-third-term-
germany

Contreras Torres, F., Pedraza Ortiz, J.E., & Mejia Restrepo, X. (2012). La mujer y el
liderazgo empresarial. Artículo de investigación, Universidad del Rosario. *Revista
diversitas – Perspectiva en psicología, 8*(1), 183-194.

De Vries, R.E., Bakker-Pieper, A., Oostenveld, W. (2009). Leadership = Communication? The relations of leaders' communication styles with leadership styles, knowledge sharing and leadership outcomes. *Journal of Business and Psychology*, *25*(3), 367-380.

Dorfman, P.W., Hanges, P.J., & Brodbeck, F.C. (2004). Leadership and cultural variation: The identification of culturally endorsed leadership profiles. In R.J. House, P.J. Hanges, M. Javidan, P.W. Dorfman, & V. Gupta (Eds.), *Culture, leadership and organizations: The GLOBE study of 62 societies* (pp. 669-719). Thousand Oaks, CA: Sage.

Eagly, A.H. (1987). Sex differences in social behavior: A social role interpretation. Hillsdale, NJ: Erlbaum.

Eagly, A.H. (1997). Sex differences in social behavior: Comparing social role theory and evolutionary psychology. *American psychologist, 50*, 1380-1383.

Eagly, A.H. & Carli, L.L. (2004). Women and men as leaders. In J. Antonakis, A.T. Cianciolo, & R. J. Sternberg (Eds.), *The nature of leaderships* (pp. 279-301). Thousand Oaks, CA: Sage Publications.

Eagly, A.H. & Carli, L.L. (2007). *Women and the labyrinth of leadership*. Harvard Business Review, September, 62-71.

Eagly, A.H., Johannesen-Schmidt, M.C. & Van Engen, M.L. (2003). Transformational, transactional and laisser faire leadership styles: A meta-analysis comparing women and men. *Psychological Bulletin, 129*, 569-591.

Eagly, A.H. & Wood, W., & Diekmann, A.B. (2000). Social role theory of sex differences and similarities: A current appraisal. In T. Eckes, & H.M. Trautner (Eds.), *The developmental social psychology of gender* (pp. 123-174). Mahwah, NJ: Erlbaum.

Ekman, P. (2005). *What the face reveals. Basic and applied studies of spontaneous expression using the Facial Action Coding System (FACS)*. New York: Oxford University Press.

Ekman, P. (2009). *Telling lies. Clues to deceit in the marketplace, politics, and marriage.* New York: W.W. Norton & Company, Inc.

Emrich, C.G., Denmark, F.L., & Den Hartog, D.N. (2004). Cross-cultural differences in gender egalitarianism. In R.J.Hanges, M.Javidan, P.W. Dorfman, & V. Gupta, (Eds.), *Culture and Organizations: the GLOBE Study of 62 Societies* (pp. 343-394) Thousand Oaks, CA: Sage Publications.

Felfe, J. (2009). *Mitarbeiterführung.* Göttingen: Hogrefe Verlag GmbH & Co. KG

Fernandez, M.P. (2006). Determinantes del diferencial salarial por género en Colombia, 1997-2003. *Desarrollo y sociedad, 58,* 165-208.

Folkman, J.R. (2006). *The power of feedback.* Hoboken NJ: Wiley & Sons Inc.

García-Retamero, R. & López-Zafra, E. (2006). Prejudice against women in male-congenial environments: Perceptions of gender role congruity in Leadership. *Sex roles, 55,* 51-61.

Gardiner, M., & Tiggemann, M. (1999). Gender differences in leadership style, job stress, and mental health in male- and female-dominated industries. *Journal of Occupational and Organizational Psychology, 72,* 301-315.

Godoy, L. & Mladinic, A. (2009). Estereotipos y roles de género en la evaluación laboral y personal de hombres y mujeres en cargos de dirección. *Psykhe, 18, 2,* 51-64.

Gupta, V., Hanges, P.J., & Dorfman, P.W. (2002). Cultural Clustering: Methodologies and findings. *Journal of World Business, 37,* 11-15.

Hall, J., & Donnell, S.M. (1979). Managerial achievement: the personal side of behavioral theory. *Human relations, 32(1),* 77-101.

Heller, T. (1982). *Women and men as leaders.* New York: Praeger.

Hill, C., Corbett, C., & Rose, A.S. (2010). *Why so few? Women in Science, Technology, Engineering and Mathematics.* Washington: AAUW. Retrieved from http://www.aauw.org/files/2013/02/Why-So-Few-Women-in-Science-Technology-Engineering-and-Mathematics.pdf

Hogan, J. & Hogan, R. (2002). Leadership and sociopolitical intelligence. In R.E. Riggio, S.E. Murphy, & F.J. Pirozzolo (Eds.), *Multiple intelligences and leadership* (pp. 75-88). Mahwah, N.J.: Lawrence Erlbaum Associates.

Hollander, E.P., & Yoder, J. (1980). Some issues in comparing women and men as leader. *Basic Applied Social Psychology, 1,* 267-280.

INE, Institut Nacional de Estadística, Notas de prensa (2011). *Producto interior bruto regional. Año 2010. Primera estimación.* Retrieved from http://www.ine.es/prensa/np645.pdf

Inter-Parliamentary Union (2013). *Women in national parliaments.* Retrieved from http://www.ipu.org/wmn-e/world.htm.

Jamieson, K.H. (1995). *Beyond the double bind. Women and leadership.* New York: Oxford University Press.

Judeh, M. (2010). Transformational leadership: A Study of gender differences in private universities. *International Review of Business Research Papers, 6, 4*, 118-125.

Kling, A. (1975). Testosterone and aggressive behaviour in men and non-human primates. In Eleftheriori B., & Spot, R. (Eds), *Hormonal correlates of behaviour* (pp. 305-323). New York: Plenum.

Kruse, L., & Wintermantel, M. (1986). Leadership Ms-Qualified: 1. The gender bias in everyday and scientific thinking. In C.F.Graumann, , & S. Moscovici (Eds.), *Changing conceptions of leadership* (pp. 171-197). New York: Springer-Verlag.

Lay, R. (1978). *Führen durch das Wort. Fremd- und Eigensteuerung, Motivation, Kommunikation, praktische Führungsdialektik.* Berlin: Ullstein Verlag.

Maccoby, E., & Jacklin, C.N. (1974). *The psychology of sex differences*. London: Oxford University Press.

McClelland, D.C. (1965). Achievement motivation can be developed. *Harvard Business Review, 43*(6), 6-24, 178.

Manning, T.T. (2002). Gender, managerial level, transformational leadership and work satisfaction. *Women in Management Review, 17*(5), 207-216.

Maruani, M. (1993). La cualificación, una construcción social sexuada. *Economía y sociología del trabajo, 21-22*, 41-50.

Mehrabian, A. (1981). *Silent messages. Implicit communication of emotions and attitudes*. Belmont: Wadsworth Publishing Company.

Moen, J.K. (1995). Women in leadership: the Norwegian example. *Journal of leadership Studies, 2*(3), 3-19.

Newport, F., & Wilke J. (2013). Americans Still Prefer a Male Boss. A plurality report that a boss' gender would make no difference. *Gullop Economy*. Retrieved from http://www.gallup.com/poll/165791/americans-prefer-male-boss.aspx

Niermeyer, R., & Postall, N. (2008). *Führen. Die erfolgreichsten Instrumente und Techniken*. Munich: Haufe Verlag.

O'Leary, V.E. (1974). Some attitudinal barriers to occupational aspirations in women. *Psychological Bulletin, 81*, 809-824.

Persky, H., Smith, K.D., & Basu, G.K. (1971). Relations of psychological measures of aggression and hostility to testosterone production in man. *Psychosomatic medicine*, 33, 265-277.

Pearce, W.B., & Cronen V. (2006). Coordinated management of meaning. In E. Griffin, (Ed.), *A first look at communication* (pp. 66-81). New York: McGraw Hill.

Powell, G.N., & Graves, L.M. (2003). *Women and men in management*. Newbury Park, CA: Sage.

Ragins, B.R., Townsend, B., & Mattis, M. (1998). Gender gap in the executive suite: CEOs and female executives report on breaking the glass ceiling. *Academy of Management Executive, 12*, 28-42.

Rosenberg, M. (2003). *Life-Enriching education: nonviolent communication helps schools improve performance, reduce conflict, and enhance relationships*. Encinitas CA: PuddleDancer Press.

Rosenberg, M. (2010). *Gewaltfreie Kommunikation. Eine Sprache des Lebens.* Paderborn: Junfermann Verlag.

Rosenberg, M. (2011). *Resolver los conflictos con la comunicación noviolenta*. Vallromanes: Alcanto S.A.

Sandberg, S. (2013). *Lean in. Women, work, and the will to lead*. London: W.H. Allen.

Schein, V.E. (1973). The relationship between sex role stereotypes and requisite management characteristics. *Journal of Applied Psychology, 57*, 95-100.

Schein, V.E. (1975). Relationships between sex role stereotypes and requisite management characteristics among female managers. *Journal of Applied Psychology, 75*(60), 340-344.

Schein, V.E. (2001). A global look of psychological barriers to women's progress in management. *Journal of Social Issues, 57*, 675-688.

Schulz von Thun, F. (2010). *Miteinander reden 1: Störungen und Klärungen. Allgemeine Psychologie der Kommunikation*. Reinbek/Hamburg: Rowohlt Taschenbuch Verlag.

Schulz von Thun, F., Ruppel, J., Stratmann, R. (2000). *Miteinander reden: Kommunikationspsychologie für Führungskräfte*. Reinbek/Hamburg: Rowohlt Taschenbuch Verlag.

Segerman-Peck, L.M. (1991). *Networking and mentoring. A woman's guide.* London: Judy Piatkus Ltd.

Seifert, C.M. (1984). Reactions to leaders: effects of sex of leader, sex of subordinate, method of leader selection and task outcome. *Dissertation Abstracts International: Section B. Sciences and Engineering, 45*(12), 3999.

Sellers, P. (2012). Fortune 500 women CEOs Hits a Milestone. *CNN Money.* Retrieved from http://postcards.blogs.fortune.cnn.com/2012/11/12/fortune-500-women-ceos-3/

Sherwin, B. (2014). Why Women Are More Effective Leaders Than Men. *Business Insider Online Edition.* Retrieved from http://www.businessinsider.com/study-women-are-better-leaders-2014-1#ixzz329HLIRkS

Stogdill, R.M. (1974). *Handbook of leadership: A survey of the literature.* New York: Free Press.

Sutton, C.D., & Moore, K.K. (1985). *Executive women – 20 years later.* Harvard Business Review, 63(5), 42-66.

Tannen, D. (1994). *Das habe ich nicht gesagt: Kommunikationsprobleme im Alltag.* Munich: GoldmannVerlag.

Tannen, D. (1996). *Talking from 9 to 5. Women and men at work: language, sex and power.* London: Virago Press.

Tharenou, P., Latimer, S., & Conroy, D., (1994). How do you make it to the top? An examination of influences on women's and men's managerial advancement. *Academy of Management Journal, 37*, 899-931.

Watzlawick, P. (2005). *Wie wirklich ist die Wirklichkeit? Wahn, Täuschung, Verstehen.* Munich: Piper Verlag GmbH.

Yañez, S. & Godoy, L. (2008). Effects of gender images and stereotypes on female E&T research careers in higher Education in Chile. In A.S. Godofroy-Genin (Ed.), *Women in engineering and technology research*. Proceedings of the PROMETEA conference. 26-27 October 2007, Paris. Zürich: Lit Verlag.

Yukl, G. (2011). *Leadership in organizations*. New Delhi: Dorling Kindersley for Pearson Education.